The Paper

Personal

Assistant

In today's digital age keeping track of voicemail messages might transition into stacks of post it notes and paper everywhere! The purpose of this book is to have a convenient resource which can be utilized across various professions as a functional grab and go tool for your business and personal needs

Date Message Checked: ____

Date Received: _______________________________________

Time Received: _______________________________________

Name: ____

Purpose of Call:

____

____

____

Notes:

____

____

____

Follow Up:

____

____

____

Date Message Checked: ____

Date Received: _______________________________________

Time Received: _______________________________________

Name: ____

Purpose of Call:

____

____

____

Notes:

____

____

____

Follow Up:

____

____

____

Date Message Checked: ____

Date Received: _______________________________

Time Received: _______________________________

Name: ____

Purpose of Call:

____

____

____

Notes:

____

____

____

Follow Up:

____

____

____

Date Message Checked: ____

Date Received: _______________________________

Time Received: _______________________________

Name: ____

Purpose of Call:

____

____

____

Notes:

____

____

____

Follow Up:

____

____

____

Date Message Checked: ____

Date Received: _______________________________

Time Received: _______________________________

Name: ____

Purpose of Call:

____

____

____

Notes:

____

____

____

Follow Up:

____

____

____

Date Message Checked: ____

Date Received: _______________________________

Time Received: _______________________________

Name: ____

Purpose of Call:

____

____

____

Notes:

____

____

____

Follow Up:

____

____

____

Date Message Checked: ____

Date Received: _______________________________

Time Received: _______________________________

Name: ____

Purpose of Call:

____

____

____

Notes:

____

____

____

Follow Up:

____

____

____

Date Message Checked: ____

Date Received: _______________________________

Time Received: _______________________________

Name: ____

Purpose of Call:

____

____

____

Notes:

____

____

____

Follow Up:

____

____

____

Date Message Checked: ____

Date Received: _______________________________

Time Received: _______________________________

Name: ____

Purpose of Call:

____

____

____

Notes:

____

____

____

Follow Up:

____

____

____

Date Message Checked: ____

Date Received: _______________________________

Time Received: _______________________________

Name: ____

Purpose of Call:

____

____

____

Notes:

____

____

____

Follow Up:

____

____

____

Date Message Checked: ____

Date Received: _______________________________

Time Received: _______________________________

Name: ____

Purpose of Call:

____

____

____

Notes:

____

____

____

Follow Up:

____

____

____

Date Message Checked: ____

Date Received: _______________________________

Time Received: _______________________________

Name: ____

Purpose of Call:

____

____

____

Notes:

____

____

____

Follow Up:

____

____

____

Date Message Checked: ____

Date Received: _______________________________

Time Received: _______________________________

Name: ____

Purpose of Call:

____

____

____

Notes:

____

____

____

Follow Up:

____

____

____

Date Message Checked: ____

Date Received: _______________________________

Time Received: _______________________________

Name: ____

Purpose of Call:

____

____

____

Notes:

____

____

____

Follow Up:

____

____

____

Date Message Checked: ____

Date Received: _________________________________

Time Received: _________________________________

Name: ____

Purpose of Call:

____

____

____

Notes:

____

____

____

Follow Up:

____

____

____

Date Message Checked: ____

Date Received: _________________________________

Time Received: _________________________________

Name: ____

Purpose of Call:

____

____

____

Notes:

____

____

____

Follow Up:

____

____

____

Date Message Checked: ____

Date Received: _______________________________

Time Received: _______________________________

Name: ____

Purpose of Call:

____

____

____

Notes:

____

____

____

Follow Up:

____

____

____

Date Message Checked: ____

Date Received: _______________________________

Time Received: _______________________________

Name: ____

Purpose of Call:

____

____

____

Notes:

____

____

____

Follow Up:

____

____

____

Date Message Checked: ____

Date Received: _______________________________

Time Received: _______________________________

Name: ____

Purpose of Call:

____

____

____

Notes:

____

____

____

Follow Up:

____

____

____

Date Message Checked: ____

Date Received: _______________________________

Time Received: _______________________________

Name: ____

Purpose of Call:

____

____

____

Notes:

____

____

____

Follow Up:

____

____

____

Date Message Checked: ____

Date Received: ___________________________________

Time Received: ___________________________________

Name: ____

Purpose of Call:

____

____

____

Notes:

____

____

____

Follow Up:

____

____

____

Date Message Checked: ____

Date Received: ___________________________________

Time Received: ___________________________________

Name: ____

Purpose of Call:

____

____

____

Notes:

____

____

____

Follow Up:

____

____

____

Date Message Checked: ____

Date Received: _______________________________

Time Received: _______________________________

Name: ____

Purpose of Call:

____

____

____

Notes:

____

____

____

Follow Up:

____

____

____

Date Message Checked: ____

Date Received: _______________________________

Time Received: _______________________________

Name: ____

Purpose of Call:

____

____

____

Notes:

____

____

____

Follow Up:

____

____

____

Date Message Checked: ____

Date Received: ______________________________

Time Received: ______________________________

Name: ____

Purpose of Call:

____

____

____

Notes:

____

____

____

Follow Up:

____

____

____

Date Message Checked: ____

Date Received: ______________________________

Time Received: ______________________________

Name: ____

Purpose of Call:

____

____

____

Notes:

____

____

____

Follow Up:

____

____

____

Date Message Checked: ____

Date Received: _____________________________

Time Received: _____________________________

Name: ____

Purpose of Call:

____

____

____

Notes:

____

____

____

Follow Up:

____

____

____

Date Message Checked: ____

Date Received: _____________________________

Time Received: _____________________________

Name: ____

Purpose of Call:

____

____

____

Notes:

____

____

____

Follow Up:

____

____

____

Date Message Checked: ____

Date Received: ________________________________

Time Received: ________________________________

Name: ____

Purpose of Call:

____

____

____

Notes:

____

____

____

Follow Up:

____

____

____

Date Message Checked: ____

Date Received: ________________________________

Time Received: ________________________________

Name: ____

Purpose of Call:

____

____

____

Notes:

____

____

____

Follow Up:

____

____

____

Date Message Checked: ____

Date Received: _________________________________

Time Received: _________________________________

Name: ____

Purpose of Call:

____

____

____

Notes:

____

____

____

Follow Up:

____

____

____

Date Message Checked: ____

Date Received: _________________________________

Time Received: _________________________________

Name: ____

Purpose of Call:

____

____

____

Notes:

____

____

____

Follow Up:

____

____

____

Date Message Checked: ____

Date Received: ______________________________

Time Received: ______________________________

Name: ____

Purpose of Call:

____

____

____

Notes:

____

____

____

Follow Up:

____

____

____

Date Message Checked: ____

Date Received: ______________________________

Time Received: ______________________________

Name: ____

Purpose of Call:

____

____

____

Notes:

____

____

____

Follow Up:

____

____

____

Date Message Checked: ____

Date Received: _______________________________

Time Received: _______________________________

Name: ____

Purpose of Call:

____

____

____

Notes:

____

____

____

Follow Up:

____

____

____

Date Message Checked: ____

Date Received: _______________________________

Time Received: _______________________________

Name: ____

Purpose of Call:

____

____

____

Notes:

____

____

____

Follow Up:

____

____

____

Date Message Checked: ____

Date Received: ______________________________

Time Received: ______________________________

Name: ____

Purpose of Call:

____

____

____

Notes:

____

____

____

Follow Up:

____

____

____

Date Message Checked: ____

Date Received: ______________________________

Time Received: ______________________________

Name: ____

Purpose of Call:

____

____

____

Notes:

____

____

____

Follow Up:

____

____

____

Date Message Checked: ____

Date Received: _______________________________

Time Received: _______________________________

Name: ____

Purpose of Call:

____

____

____

Notes:

____

____

____

Follow Up:

____

____

____

Date Message Checked: ____

Date Received: _______________________________

Time Received: _______________________________

Name: ____

Purpose of Call:

____

____

____

Notes:

____

____

____

Follow Up:

____

____

____

Date Message Checked: ____

Date Received: _________________________________

Time Received: _________________________________

Name: ____

Purpose of Call:

____

____

____

Notes:

____

____

____

Follow Up:

____

____

____

Date Message Checked: ____

Date Received: _________________________________

Time Received: _________________________________

Name: ____

Purpose of Call:

____

____

____

Notes:

____

____

____

Follow Up:

____

____

____

Date Message Checked: ____

Date Received: _______________________________

Time Received: _______________________________

Name: ____

Purpose of Call:

____

____

____

Notes:

____

____

____

Follow Up:

____

____

____

Date Message Checked: ____

Date Received: _______________________________

Time Received: _______________________________

Name: ____

Purpose of Call:

____

____

____

Notes:

____

____

____

Follow Up:

____

____

____

Date Message Checked: ____

Date Received: _______________________________

Time Received: _______________________________

Name: ____

Purpose of Call:

____

____

____

Notes:

____

____

____

Follow Up:

____

____

____

Date Message Checked: ____

Date Received: _______________________________

Time Received: _______________________________

Name: ____

Purpose of Call:

____

____

____

Notes:

____

____

____

Follow Up:

____

____

____

Date Message Checked: ____

Date Received: _______________________________

Time Received: _______________________________

Name: ____

Purpose of Call:

____

____

____

Notes:

____

____

____

Follow Up:

____

____

____

Date Message Checked: ____

Date Received: _______________________________

Time Received: _______________________________

Name: ____

Purpose of Call:

____

____

____

Notes:

____

____

____

Follow Up:

____

____

____

Date Message Checked: ____

Date Received: _______________________________

Time Received: _______________________________

Name: ____

Purpose of Call:

____

____

____

Notes:

____

____

____

Follow Up:

____

____

____

Date Message Checked: ____

Date Received: _______________________________

Time Received: _______________________________

Name: ____

Purpose of Call:

____

____

____

Notes:

____

____

____

Follow Up:

____

____

____

Date Message Checked: ____

Date Received: ______________________________

Time Received: ______________________________

Name: ____

Purpose of Call:

____

____

____

Notes:

____

____

____

Follow Up:

____

____

____

Date Message Checked: ____

Date Received: ______________________________

Time Received: ______________________________

Name: ____

Purpose of Call:

____

____

____

Notes:

____

____

____

Follow Up:

____

____

____

Date Message Checked: ____

Date Received: _______________________________

Time Received: _______________________________

Name: ____

Purpose of Call:

____

____

____

Notes:

____

____

____

Follow Up:

____

____

____

Date Message Checked: ____

Date Received: _______________________________

Time Received: _______________________________

Name: ____

Purpose of Call:

____

____

____

Notes:

____

____

____

Follow Up:

____

____

____

Date Message Checked: ____

Date Received: ______________________________

Time Received: ______________________________

Name: ____

Purpose of Call:

____

____

____

Notes:

____

____

____

Follow Up:

____

____

____

Date Message Checked: ____

Date Received: ______________________________

Time Received: ______________________________

Name: ____

Purpose of Call:

____

____

____

Notes:

____

____

____

Follow Up:

____

____

____

Date Message Checked: ____

Date Received: _________________________________

Time Received: _________________________________

Name: ____

Purpose of Call:

____

____

____

Notes:

____

____

____

Follow Up:

____

____

____

Date Message Checked: ____

Date Received: _________________________________

Time Received: _________________________________

Name: ____

Purpose of Call:

____

____

____

Notes:

____

____

____

Follow Up:

____

____

Date Message Checked: ____

Date Received: _______________________________

Time Received: _______________________________

Name: ____

Purpose of Call:

____

____

____

Notes:

____

____

____

Follow Up:

____

____

____

Date Message Checked: ____

Date Received: _______________________________

Time Received: _______________________________

Name: ____

Purpose of Call:

____

____

____

Notes:

____

____

____

Follow Up:

____

____

____

Date Message Checked: ____

Date Received: _________________________________

Time Received: _________________________________

Name: ____

Purpose of Call:

____

____

____

Notes:

____

____

____

Follow Up:

____

____

____

Date Message Checked: ____

Date Received: _________________________________

Time Received: _________________________________

Name: ____

Purpose of Call:

____

____

____

Notes:

____

____

____

Follow Up:

____

____

____

Date Message Checked: ____

Date Received: _______________________________

Time Received: _______________________________

Name: ____

Purpose of Call:

____

____

____

Notes:

____

____

____

Follow Up:

____

____

____

Date Message Checked: ____

Date Received: _______________________________

Time Received: _______________________________

Name: ____

Purpose of Call:

____

____

____

Notes:

____

____

____

Follow Up:

____

____

____

Date Message Checked: ____

Date Received: _______________________________

Time Received: _______________________________

Name: ____

Purpose of Call:

____

____

____

Notes:

____

____

____

Follow Up:

____

____

____

Date Message Checked: ____

Date Received: _______________________________

Time Received: _______________________________

Name: ____

Purpose of Call:

____

____

____

Notes:

____

____

____

Follow Up:

____

____

____

Date Message Checked: ____

Date Received: _______________________________

Time Received: _______________________________

Name: ____

Purpose of Call:

____

____

____

Notes:

____

____

____

Follow Up:

____

____

____

Date Message Checked: ____

Date Received: _______________________________

Time Received: _______________________________

Name: ____

Purpose of Call:

____

____

____

Notes:

____

____

____

Follow Up:

____

____

____

Date Message Checked: ____

Date Received: _________________________________

Time Received: _________________________________

Name: ____

Purpose of Call:

____

____

____

Notes:

____

____

____

Follow Up:

____

____

____

Date Message Checked: ____

Date Received: _________________________________

Time Received: _________________________________

Name: ____

Purpose of Call:

____

____

____

Notes:

____

____

____

Follow Up:

____

____

____

Date Message Checked: ____

Date Received: ___________________________

Time Received: ___________________________

Name: ____

Purpose of Call:

____

____

____

Notes:

____

____

____

Follow Up:

____

____

____

Date Message Checked: ____

Date Received: ___________________________

Time Received: ___________________________

Name: ____

Purpose of Call:

____

____

____

Notes:

____

____

____

Follow Up:

____

____

____

Date Message Checked: ____

Date Received: _____________________________

Time Received: _____________________________

Name: ____

Purpose of Call:

____

____

____

Notes:

____

____

____

Follow Up:

____

____

____

Date Message Checked: ____

Date Received: _____________________________

Time Received: _____________________________

Name: ____

Purpose of Call:

____

____

____

Notes:

____

____

____

Follow Up:

____

____

____

Date Message Checked: ____

Date Received: ___________________________

Time Received: ___________________________

Name: ____

Purpose of Call:

____

____

____

Notes:

____

____

____

Follow Up:

____

____

____

Date Message Checked: ____

Date Received: ___________________________

Time Received: ___________________________

Name: ____

Purpose of Call:

____

____

____

Notes:

____

____

____

Follow Up:

____

____

____

Date Message Checked: ____

Date Received: _______________________________

Time Received: _______________________________

Name: ____

Purpose of Call:

____

____

____

Notes:

____

____

____

Follow Up:

____

____

____

Date Message Checked: ____

Date Received: _______________________________

Time Received: _______________________________

Name: ____

Purpose of Call:

____

____

____

Notes:

____

____

____

Follow Up:

____

____

____

Date Message Checked: ____

Date Received: _______________________________

Time Received: _______________________________

Name: ____

Purpose of Call:

____

____

____

Notes:

____

____

____

Follow Up:

____

____

____

Date Message Checked: ____

Date Received: _______________________________

Time Received: _______________________________

Name: ____

Purpose of Call:

____

____

____

Notes:

____

____

____

Follow Up:

____

____

____

Date Message Checked: ____

Date Received: ___________________________________

Time Received: ___________________________________

Name: ____

Purpose of Call:

____

____

____

Notes:

____

____

____

Follow Up:

____

____

____

Date Message Checked: ____

Date Received: ___________________________________

Time Received: ___________________________________

Name: ____

Purpose of Call:

____

____

____

Notes:

____

____

____

Follow Up:

____

____

____

Date Message Checked: ____
Date Received: _______________________________
Time Received: _______________________________
Name: ____

Purpose of Call:

____
____
____

Notes:

____
____
____

Follow Up:

____
____
____

Date Message Checked: ____
Date Received: _______________________________
Time Received: _______________________________
Name: ____

Purpose of Call:

____
____
____

Notes:

____
____
____

Follow Up:

____
____
____

Date Message Checked: ____

Date Received: ______________________________

Time Received: ______________________________

Name: ____

Purpose of Call:

____

____

____

Notes:

____

____

____

Follow Up:

____

____

____

Date Message Checked: ____

Date Received: ______________________________

Time Received: ______________________________

Name: ____

Purpose of Call:

____

____

____

Notes:

____

____

____

Follow Up:

____

____

____

Date Message Checked: ____
Date Received: ______________________________
Time Received: ______________________________
Name: ____

Purpose of Call:

____
____
____

Notes:

____
____
____

Follow Up:

____
____
____

Date Message Checked: ____
Date Received: ______________________________
Time Received: ______________________________
Name: ____

Purpose of Call:

____
____
____

Notes:

____
____
____

Follow Up:

____
____
____

Date Message Checked: ____

Date Received: ___________________________

Time Received: ___________________________

Name: ____

Purpose of Call:

____

____

____

Notes:

____

____

____

Follow Up:

____

____

____

Date Message Checked: ____

Date Received: ___________________________

Time Received: ___________________________

Name: ____

Purpose of Call:

____

____

____

Notes:

____

____

____

Follow Up:

____

____

____

Date Message Checked: ____

Date Received: _______________________________

Time Received: _______________________________

Name: ____

Purpose of Call:

____

____

____

Notes:

____

____

____

Follow Up:

____

____

____

Date Message Checked: ____

Date Received: _______________________________

Time Received: _______________________________

Name: ____

Purpose of Call:

____

____

____

Notes:

____

____

____

Follow Up:

____

____

____

Date Message Checked: ____

Date Received: ___________________________________

Time Received: ___________________________________

Name: ____

Purpose of Call:

____

____

____

Notes:

____

____

____

Follow Up:

____

____

____

Date Message Checked: ____

Date Received: ___________________________________

Time Received: ___________________________________

Name: ____

Purpose of Call:

____

____

____

Notes:

____

____

____

Follow Up:

____

____

____

Date Message Checked: ____

Date Received: _______________________________

Time Received: _______________________________

Name: ____

Purpose of Call:

____

____

____

Notes:

____

____

____

Follow Up:

____

____

____

Date Message Checked: ____

Date Received: _______________________________

Time Received: _______________________________

Name: ____

Purpose of Call:

____

____

____

Notes:

____

____

____

Follow Up:

____

____

____

Date Message Checked: _______________________________________

Date Received: _______________________________

Time Received: _______________________________

Name: _______________________________________

Purpose of Call:

____

____

____

Notes:

____

____

____

Follow Up:

____

____

____

Date Message Checked: _______________________________________

Date Received: _______________________________

Time Received: _______________________________

Name: _______________________________________

Purpose of Call:

____

____

____

Notes:

____

____

____

Follow Up:

____

____

____

Date Message Checked: ____

Date Received: _______________________________

Time Received: _______________________________

Name: ____

Purpose of Call:

____

____

____

Notes:

____

____

____

Follow Up:

____

____

____

Date Message Checked: ____

Date Received: _______________________________

Time Received: _______________________________

Name: ____

Purpose of Call:

____

____

____

Notes:

____

____

____

Follow Up:

____

____

____

Date Message Checked: ____

Date Received: _______________________________

Time Received: _______________________________

Name: ____

Purpose of Call:

____

____

____

Notes:

____

____

____

Follow Up:

____

____

____

Date Message Checked: ____

Date Received: _______________________________

Time Received: _______________________________

Name: ____

Purpose of Call:

____

____

____

Notes:

____

____

____

Follow Up:

____

____

____

Date Message Checked: ____

Date Received: _______________________________

Time Received: _______________________________

Name: ____

Purpose of Call:

____

____

____

Notes:

____

____

____

Follow Up:

____

____

____

Date Message Checked: ____

Date Received: _______________________________

Time Received: _______________________________

Name: ____

Purpose of Call:

____

____

____

Notes:

____

____

____

Follow Up:

____

____

____

Date Message Checked: ____

Date Received: _______________________________

Time Received: _______________________________

Name: ____

Purpose of Call:

____

____

____

Notes:

____

____

____

Follow Up:

____

____

____

Date Message Checked: ____

Date Received: _______________________________

Time Received: _______________________________

Name: ____

Purpose of Call:

____

____

____

Notes:

____

____

____

Follow Up:

____

____

____

Date Message Checked: ____

Date Received: _______________________________

Time Received: _______________________________

Name: ____

Purpose of Call:

____

____

____

Notes:

____

____

____

Follow Up:

____

____

____

Date Message Checked: ____

Date Received: _______________________________

Time Received: _______________________________

Name: ____

Purpose of Call:

____

____

____

Notes:

____

____

____

Follow Up:

____

____

____

Date Message Checked: ____

Date Received: _______________________________

Time Received: _______________________________

Name: ____

Purpose of Call:

____

____

____

Notes:

____

____

____

Follow Up:

____

____

____

Date Message Checked: ____

Date Received: _______________________________

Time Received: _______________________________

Name: ____

Purpose of Call:

____

____

____

Notes:

____

____

____

Follow Up:

____

____

____

Date Message Checked: ____

Date Received: ______________________________

Time Received: ______________________________

Name: ____

Purpose of Call:

____

____

____

Notes:

____

____

____

Follow Up:

____

____

____

Date Message Checked: ____

Date Received: ______________________________

Time Received: ______________________________

Name: ____

Purpose of Call:

____

____

____

Notes:

____

____

____

Follow Up:

____

____

____

Date Message Checked: ____

Date Received: _______________________________

Time Received: _______________________________

Name: ____

Purpose of Call:

____

____

____

Notes:

____

____

____

Follow Up:

____

____

____

Date Message Checked: ____

Date Received: _______________________________

Time Received: _______________________________

Name: ____

Purpose of Call:

____

____

____

Notes:

____

____

____

Follow Up:

____

____

____

www.ingramcontent.com/pod-product-compliance
Lightning Source LLC
Chambersburg PA
CBHW080814280726
48660CB00018B/3440